Handwriting Without Tears®

Name:

MW00998294

Cursive Success

tower

boat

trumpet

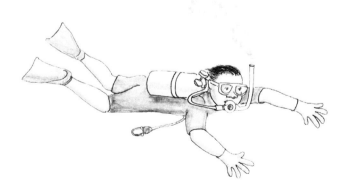

Galileo

diver

Jupiter

Handwriting Without Tears®

8001 MacArthur Blvd
Cabin John, MD 20818
301.263.2700
www.hwtears.com

Author and Illustrator: Jan Z. Olsen, OTR
HWT Adviser: Emily F. Knapton, M.Ed., OTR/L
HWT Graphic Designers: Julie Koborg and Scott Routson

January 3, 2013

Dear Student,

   Can you read this? It's cursive. Cursive is connected handwriting. Students like the way it makes their writing look more grown up.

   At first, cursive takes more time, but with practice you'll find it faster than print and just as neat. As you master cursive, you will develop your own personal style. I hope you enjoy this book.

   Sincerely,
   Jan Z. Olsen

Uu Bb Cc Dd Ee Ff Gg Hh Ii Jj Kk Ll Mm
9   36   8   10   15   17   11   12   24   25   28   16   44

TABLE OF CONTENTS

Getting Started

Preparing for Cursive

Lowercase Letters

Lowercase Lessons

c a d g h t p e l f

Lowercase Lessons u y i j

Lowercase Lessons k r s

Lowercase Lessons o w b v

Nn Oo Pp 2q Rr Ss Tt Uu Vv Ww Xx Yy Zz

45 34 14 51 29 30 13 22 37 35 50 23 52

Capitals

Key to Writing Activities

Cursive Capitals & Lowercase Letters

Aa Bb Cc Dd Ee Ff Gg

Hh Ii Jj Kk Ll Mm

Nn Oo Pp Qq Rr Ss Tt

Uu Vv Ww Xx Yy Zz

Print Capitals & Lowercase Letters

Aa Bb Cc Dd Ee Ff Gg

Hh Ii Jj Kk Ll Mm

Nn Oo Pp Qq Rr Ss Tt

Uu Vv Ww Xx Yy Zz

Learn & Check

Learn letters, words, sentences, and how to check them.
When you see the box ☐, it's time to check your work.

☑ **Check letter** Teachers: Help children ☑ their letter for correct Start, Steps, and Bump.

1. Start correctly.

2. Do each step.

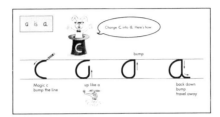

3. Bump the lines.

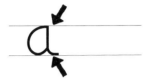

☑ **Check word** Teachers: Help children ☑ their word for correct letter Size, Placement, and Connections.

1. Make letters the correct size.
2. Place letters correctly: tall, small, or descending.

3. Connect letters correctly.

Tall   **Small**   **Descending**

☑ **Check sentence** Teachers: Help children ☑ their sentence for correct Capitalization, Word Spacing, and Ending Punctuation.

1. Start with a capital.

2. Put space between words.

3. End with **.** **?** or **!**

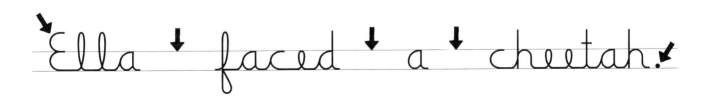

Paper Placement & Pencil Skills

LEFT-HANDED

Place the **left** corner higher.

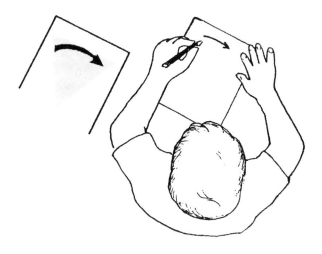

RIGHT-HANDED

Place the **right** corner higher.

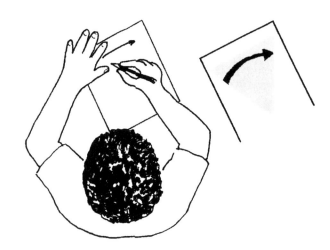

Standard grip: Hold pencil with
thumb + index finger.
Pencil rests on middle finger.

Eraser points to **left** shoulder.

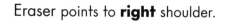

Eraser points to **right** shoulder.

Alternate grip: Hold pencil with
thumb + index and middle fingers.
Pencil rests on ring finger.

Cursive Warm-Ups

Under and over   **Up and straight down**   **Up and loop down**   **Descending loop**

Start on the star. Do one row a day.

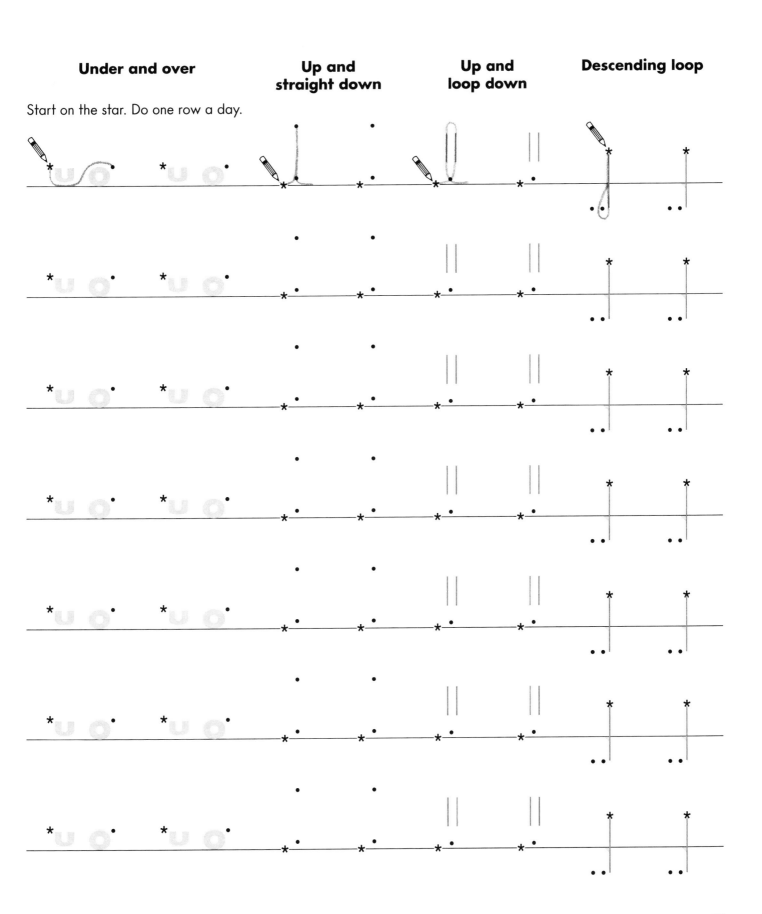

c is c

Hi! I'm the Magic C Bunny. I'll show you how to connect c to c.

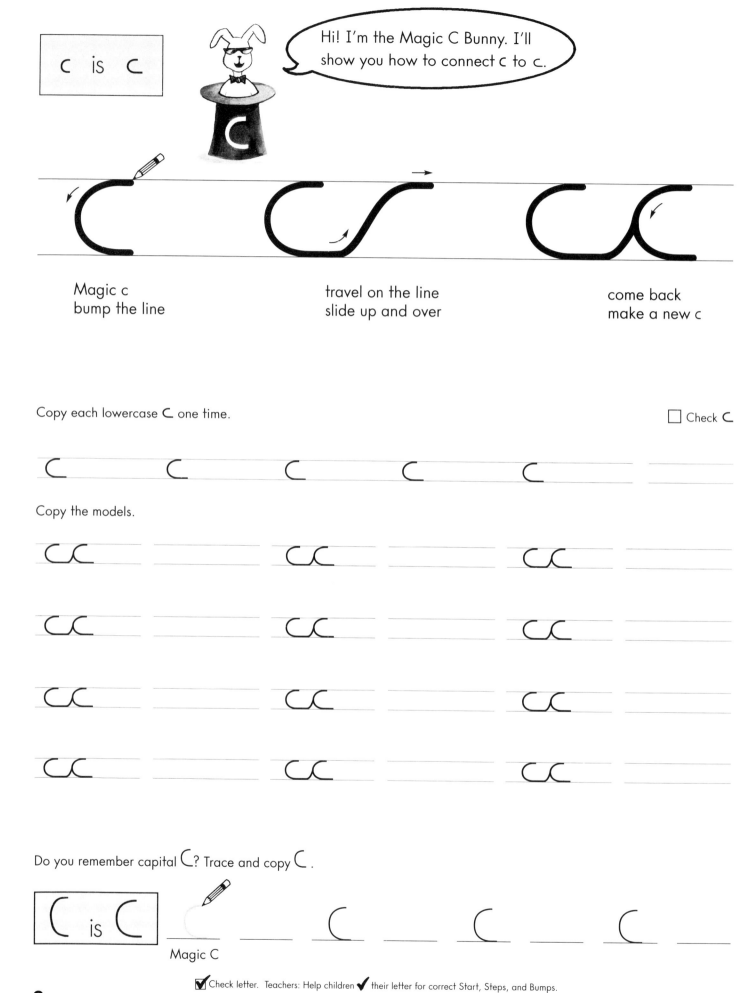

Magic c
bump the line

travel on the line
slide up and over

come back
make a new c

Copy each lowercase c one time.

☐ Check c

Copy the models.

Do you remember capital C? Trace and copy C.

c is C

Magic C

☑ Check letter. Teachers: Help children ✔ their letter for correct Start, Steps, and Bumps.

© 2013 Handwriting Without Tears®

a is a

Change c into a. Here's how:

bump

Magic c
bump the line

up like a

back down
bump
travel away

Copy each lowercase a one time.

☐ Check a

a   a   a   a   a

Copy the models.

aa   aa   aa

ac   ac   ac

ac   ac   ac

ca   ca   ca

Do you remember capital a? Trace and copy a.

A is a

Magic C   up   back
                 down

d is d

Now change c into d.

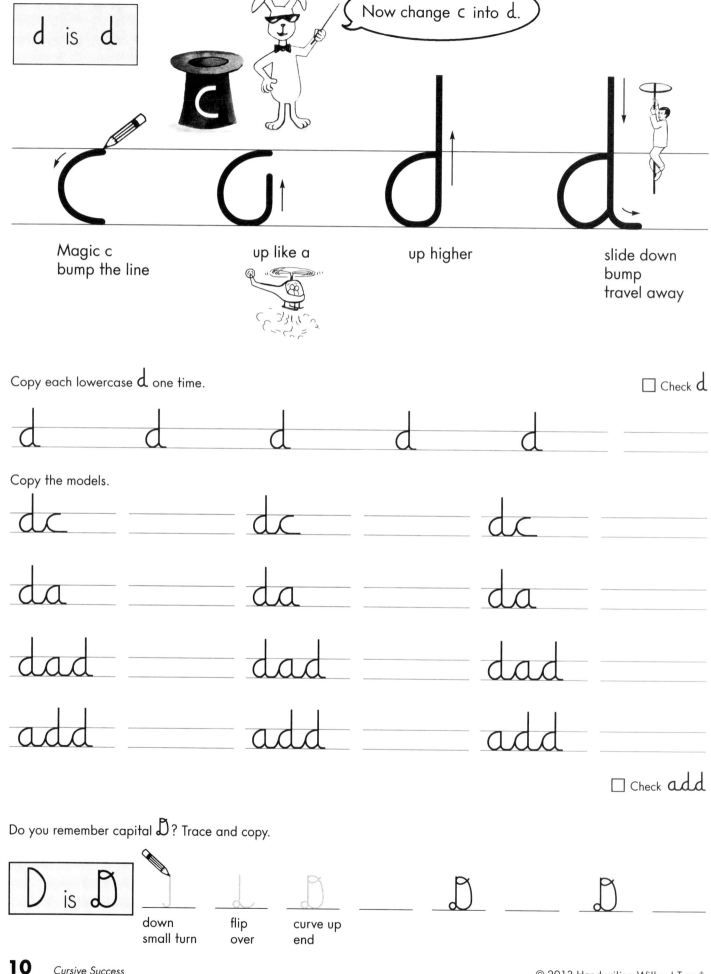

Magic c
bump the line

up like a

up higher

slide down
bump
travel away

Copy each lowercase d one time.

☐ Check d

d   d   d   d   d

Copy the models.

dc   dc   dc

da   da   da

dad   dad   dad

add   add   add

☐ Check add

Do you remember capital D? Trace and copy.

D is D

down
small turn

flip
over

curve up
end

g is g

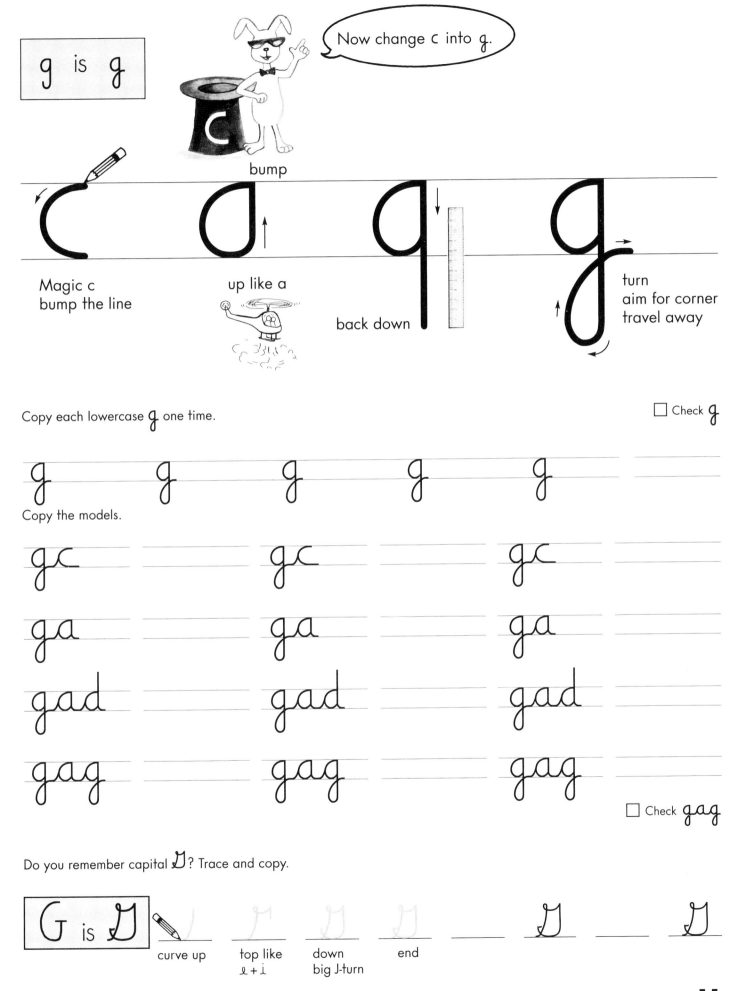

Now change c into g.

bump

Magic c
bump the line

up like a

back down

turn
aim for corner
travel away

Copy each lowercase g one time.   ☐ Check g

g   g   g   g   g

Copy the models.

gc   gc   gc

ga   ga   ga

gad   gad   gad

gag   gag   gag

☐ Check gag

Do you remember capital G? Trace and copy.

G is G

curve up   top like   down   end
            ℓ + i   big J-turn

Cursive Success

h is h

travel
up like a

slide down
bump

climb back up
and over

and down
bump
travel away

Copy h.   ☐ Check h

h   h   h   h   h

Copy the models.

ha   ha   ha

ah   ah   ah

cha   cha   cha

had   had   had

☐ Check had

Do you remember capital H? Trace and copy.

H is H

ready
down

down

up
over

end

H   H

t is t

Left-handed?
You may cross this way.

travel
up like a

slide down
bump
travel away

cross

Copy t .

☐ Check t

t   t   t   t   t

Copy the words.

that _____ that _____

chat _____ chat _____

catch _____ catch _____

data _____ data _____

☐ Check data

Do you remember capital J? Trace and copy.

T is J

ready
down

J-turn

J   J   J   J

☑ Check word. Teachers: Help children ✔ their letter for correct Start, Steps, and Bumps.

© 2013 Handwriting Without Tears®

Cursive Success **13**

p is p

Be sure to stay on the pole when you climb back up.

bump

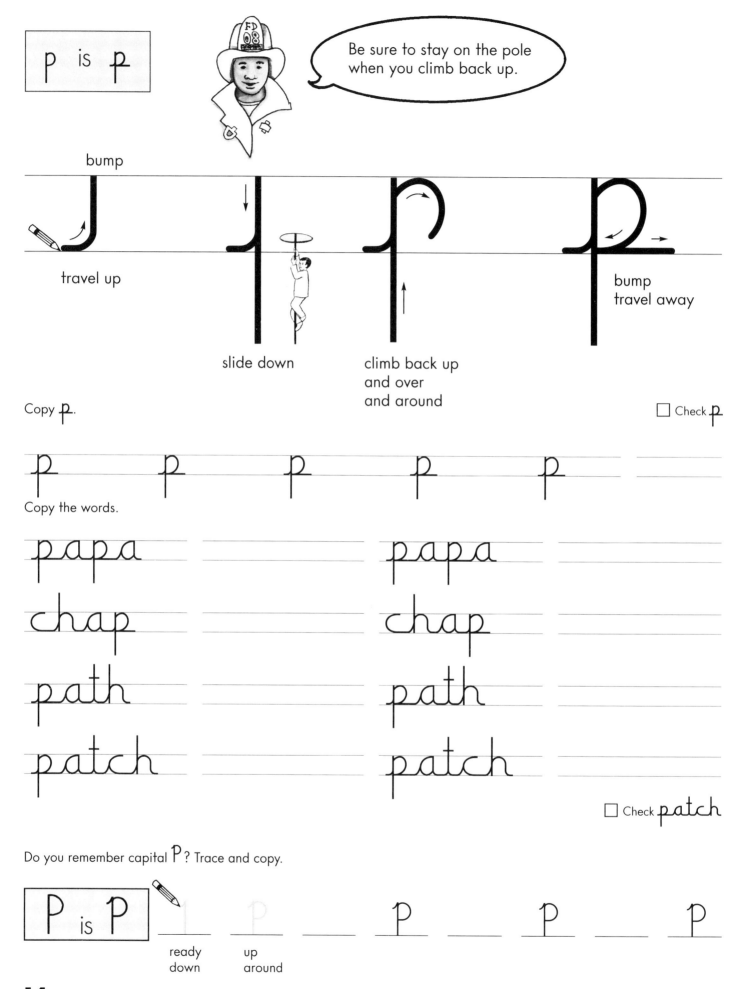

travel up

slide down

climb back up
and over
and around

bump
travel away

Copy p.   □ Check p

p   p   p   p   p

Copy the words.

papa   papa

chap   chap

path   path

patch   patch

□ Check patch

Do you remember capital P? Trace and copy.

P is P   P   P   P   P

ready   up
down   around

e is l

Name that letter!
It's _____.

bump

travel
then up

turn

down
stay on your side
bump
travel away

Copy l.   ☐ Check l

l   l   l   l   l

Copy the words.

each   each

tepee   tepee

page   page

etc.   etc.

☐ Check etc.

Do you remember capital Ɛ? Trace and copy.

E is Ɛ   Ɛ   Ɛ   Ɛ   Ɛ
                c in the air   c again

l is 𝓁

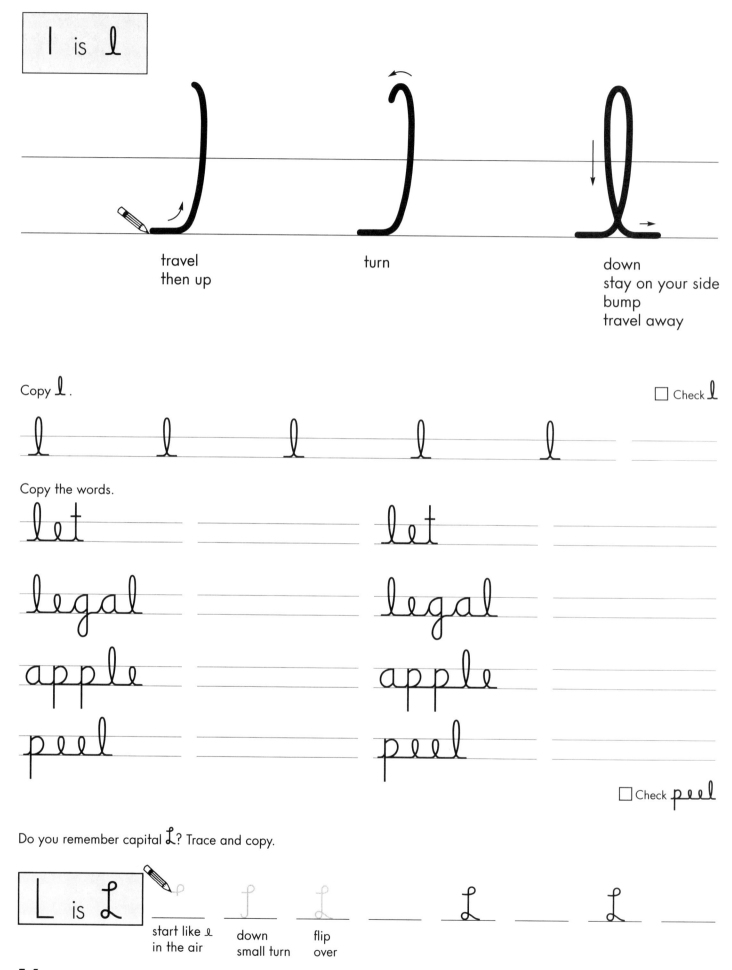

travel
then up

turn

down
stay on your side
bump
travel away

Copy 𝓁 .   ☐ Check 𝓁

Copy the words.

let   let

legal   legal

apple   apple

peel   peel

☐ Check peel

Do you remember capital 𝓛? Trace and copy.

L is 𝓛

start like 𝓁   down   flip
in the air   small turn   over

f is f

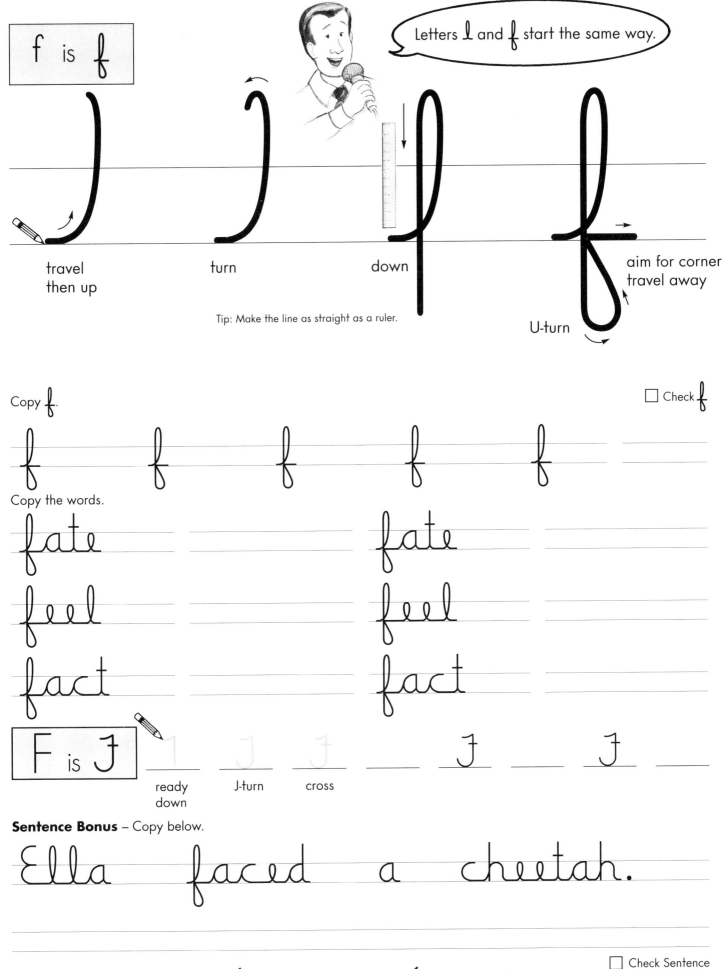

Letters l and f start the same way.

travel
then up

turn

Tip: Make the line as straight as a ruler.

down

U-turn

aim for corner
travel away

Copy f.

☐ Check f

f   f   f   f   f

Copy the words.

fate   fate

feel   feel

fact   fact

F is J

ready
down

J-turn

cross

J   J

J   J

Sentence Bonus – Copy below.

Ella   faced   a   cheetah.

© 2013 Handwriting Without Tears®

✓ Check sentence. Teachers: Help children ✔ their letter for correct Capitalization,
Word Spacing, and Ending Punctuation.

☐ Check Sentence

Cursive Success **17**

Review & Mastery: Cursive to Cursive

a b c d e f g h i j k l m
n o p q r s t u v w x y z

Wait for the teacher to play The Freeze Game. Directions are on the next page.

get — let

fat — cat

had — pad

led — fed

peg — leg

tag — lag

tap — cap

fad — lad

pet — ape

gag — lag

tea — pea

fee — gee

See — Teacher's Guide page 64.

Directions: You have learned 10 cursive letters. That's enough to play The Freeze Game.

1. Teacher calls out, "Pencils in the air and circle, circle, circle over the page."
2. "Freeze! Now lower your pencil slowly down onto the page."
3. "Copy the word closest to your pencil. Copy its partner word, too."
4. Play The Freeze Game again.

Challenging

that – chat

dead – heat

held – help

felt – pelt

feet – feel

late – fate

More Challenging

decade   attach   heated

patched   defeated   paddled

a b c d e f g h i j k l m
n o p q r s t u v w x y z

Translate print into cursive.

flag → flag

Directions: This lesson isn't about translating one language into another, but translating print into cursive.

1. For lines 1-10, translate the print words into cursive.
2. Every word uses one more letter.
3. You can work up to a ten-letter word.
4. For lines 11 and 12, think of words that use only the letters that have been taught.
5. Write them out in print.
6. Then translate the printed word into cursive. (You can also swap books with a friend so you can translate each other's words.)

1. f   f

2. at

3. cap

4. flag

5. place

6. called

7. fetched

8. accepted

9. delegated

10. tattletale

11.

12.

Wait for the teacher to spell the words.
Write the Silly Spelling Words in cursive.

1. _____

2. _____

3. _____

4. _____

5. _____

6. _____

7. _____

8. _____

9. _____

10. _____

Extreme Challenge

_____

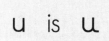

↓
tug

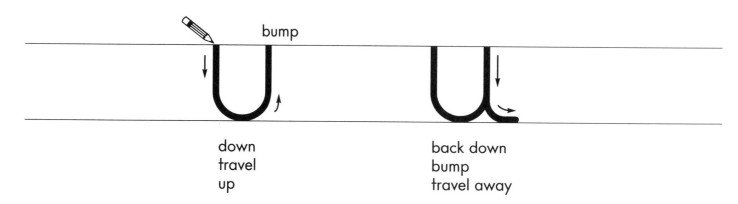

bump

down
travel
up

back down
bump
travel away

Copy u.   ☐ Check u

u   u   u   u   u

Copy the words.

up   up

tug   tug

glue   glue

laugh   laugh

                                                          ☐ Check laugh

Do you remember capital U? Trace and copy.

U is U   down   back   U   U   U
                travel, up   down

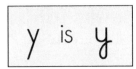 y is y

 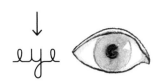

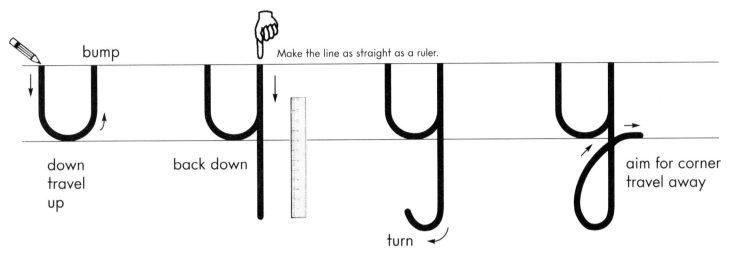

bump   Make the line as straight as a ruler.

down   back down   aim for corner
travel   travel away
up

turn

Copy y.   ☐ Check y

Copy the words.

yell   yell

fly   fly

happy   happy

eye   eye

☐ Check eye

Do you remember capital Y? Trace and copy.

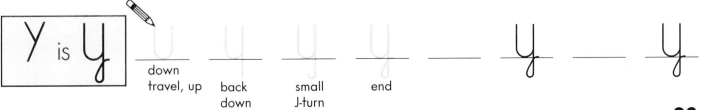

Y is Y   down   back   small   end
                travel, up   down   J-turn

i is i

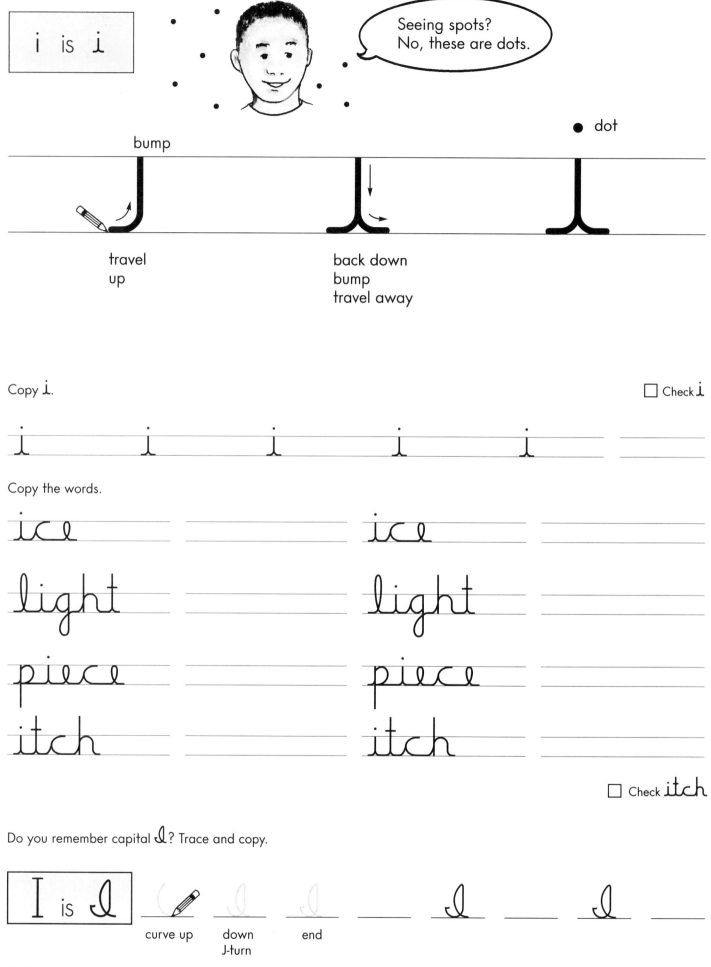

Seeing spots?
No, these are dots.

• dot

bump

travel
up

back down
bump
travel away

Copy i.   ☐ Check i

i   i   i   i   i

Copy the words.

ice   ice

light   light

piece   piece

itch   itch

☐ Check itch

Do you remember capital I? Trace and copy.

I is I   ✏   I   I   I   I

curve up   down   end
            J-turn

j is j

Seeing spots?
No, these are dots.

• dot

bump
travel up
back down
turn
aim for corner
travel away

Copy j.

☐ Check j

j   j   j   j   j

Copy the words.

jeep   jeep

judge   judge

eject   eject

J is J

curve up   straight down   small J-turn   end

J   J

Sentence Bonus – Copy below.

Jay had papaya juice.

☐ Check Sentence

© 2013 Handwriting Without Tears®

Cursive Success **25**

Review & Mastery: Cursive to Cursive

a ___ c d e f g h i j ___ l ___

___ ___ o p ___ ___ ___ t u ___ ___ y ___

Wait for the teacher to play The Freeze Game.

cut   -   cute

life   -   lift

jay   -   pay

tail   -   jail

full   -   pull

light   -   tight

field   -   yield

guppy   -   puppy

fact   -   tact

itch   -   pitch

playful   athletic   helpful

See — Teacher's Guide page 72.

Print to Cursive

up → up

Translate print into cursive.
For lines 11 and 12, make new words with letters you've learned.

1. u i y j   u i y j
2. up
3. fit
4. jail
5. eight
6. played
7. delight
8. actually
9. difficult
10. delightful
11.
12.

Spelling to Cursive

juicy, j-u-i-c-y

Wait for the teacher to spell the words.
Write the Silly Spelling Words in cursive.

1.
2.
3.
4.
5.
6.
7.
8.
9.
10.

Extreme Challenge

k is k

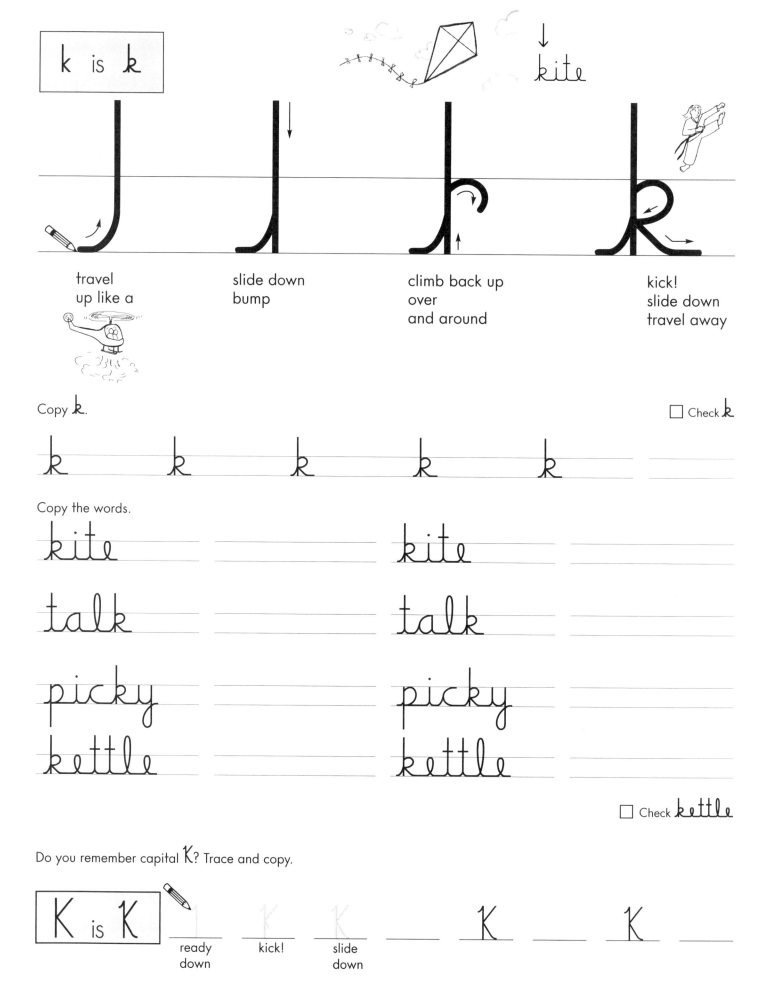

↓ kite

travel
up like a

slide down
bump

climb back up
over
and around

kick!
slide down
travel away

Copy k.   ☐ Check k

k   k   k   k   k

Copy the words.

kite _____   kite _____

talk _____   talk _____

picky _____   picky _____

kettle _____   kettle _____

                                              ☐ Check kettle

Do you remember capital K? Trace and copy.

K is K ✏ ___ J ___ K ___ K ___ K ___ K ___
        ready   kick!   slide
        down   down

© 2013 Handwriting Without Tears®

r is ℳ

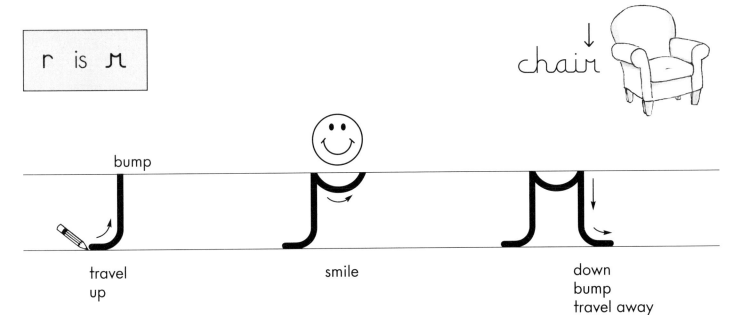

chair

bump

travel
up

smile

down
bump
travel away

Copy ℳ.   ☐ Check ℳ

Copy the words.

raft   raft

chair   chair

radar   radar

there   there

☐ Check there

Do you remember capital R? Trace and copy.

R is R

ready   up   slide
down   around   down

s is _s_

↓ sail

bump

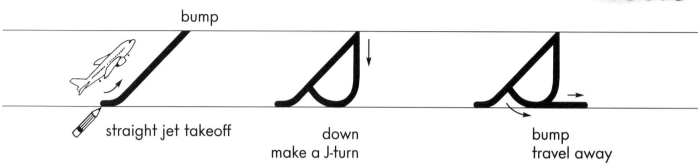
straight jet takeoff

down
make a J-turn

bump
travel away

Copy _s_ .   ☐ Check _s_

_s_   _s_   _s_   _s_   _s_

Copy the words.

she   she

sail   sail

fast   fast

S is _S_   straight   print S   end   _S_   _S_
           jet takeoff

Sentence Bonus – Copy below.

Sharks' teeth are sharp.

                                                                        ☐ Check Sentence

TRANSLATE NAMES

Translate these printed names into cursive. Connect the capital to the next letter.

Ashley	Charlie	Julie	Eric
Yates	Luke	Rachel	Kyle
Ella	Ali	Lily	Jake
Kayla	Ulysses	Chelsea	Rick

Translate these printed names into cursive. DO NOT connect the capital to the next letter.

Grace	Isaac	Sarah	Tyler
Hailey	Paul	Deliah	Fred

Review & Mastery: Cursive to Cursive

a _b_ c d e f g h i j _k_ l _m_

_m_ _o_ p _q_ r s t u _v_ _w_ _x_ y _z_

Wait for the teacher to play The Freeze Game.

pick   -   trick   fake   -   shake

rest   -   guest   here   -   there

luck   -   truck   raft   -   craft

race   -   trace   icy   -   juicy

rash   -   trash   fries   -   tries

yesterday   straight   surprised

See — Teacher's Guide page 78.   © 2013 Handwriting Without Tears®

as → as

risk, r-i-s-k

Translate print into cursive.
For lines 11 and 12, make new words with letters you've learned.

Wait for the teacher to spell the words.
Write the Silly Spelling Words in cursive.

1. k r s   k r a

2. as

3. kid

4. park

5. skate

6. repeat

7. traffic

8. straight

9. scratched

10. artificial

11.

12.

1.

2.

3.

4.

5.

6.

7.

8.

9.

10.

Extreme Challenge

o is σ

Magic c   keep on   circle around   end with a tow
                 going

Copy σ.   ☐ Check σ

σ   σ   σ   σ

Copy the words.

ouch   ouch

cloud   cloud

proud   proud

coat   coat

☐ Check coat

Do you remember capital O? Trace and copy.

O is O   Magic C   keep on   end   O   O
                           going

w is ⅏

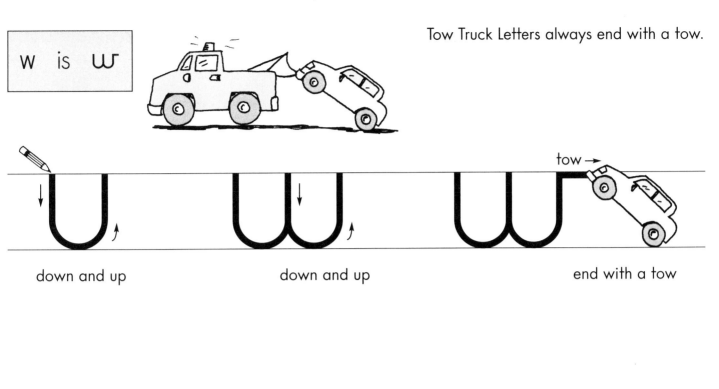

down and up   down and up   end with a tow

Copy ⅏.   ☐ Check ⅏

Copy the words.

wash ___ ___   wash ___ ___

would ___ ___   would ___ ___

claw ___ ___   claw ___ ___

flew ___ ___   flew ___ ___

☐ Check flew

Do you remember capital ⅏? Trace and copy.

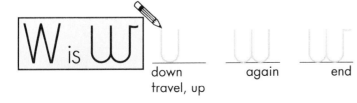

W is ⅏   down travel, up   again   end

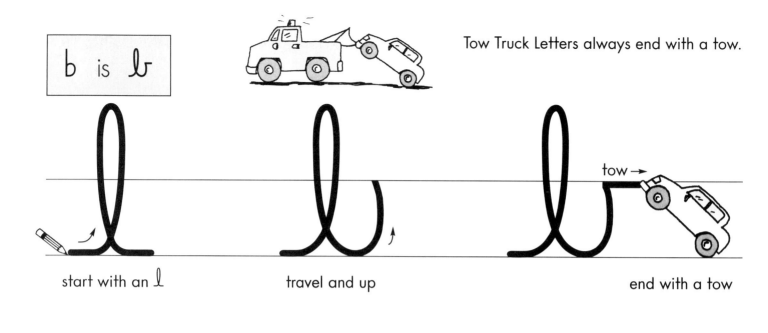

b is ♭

start with an ℓ

travel and up

Tow Truck Letters always end with a tow.

tow →

end with a tow

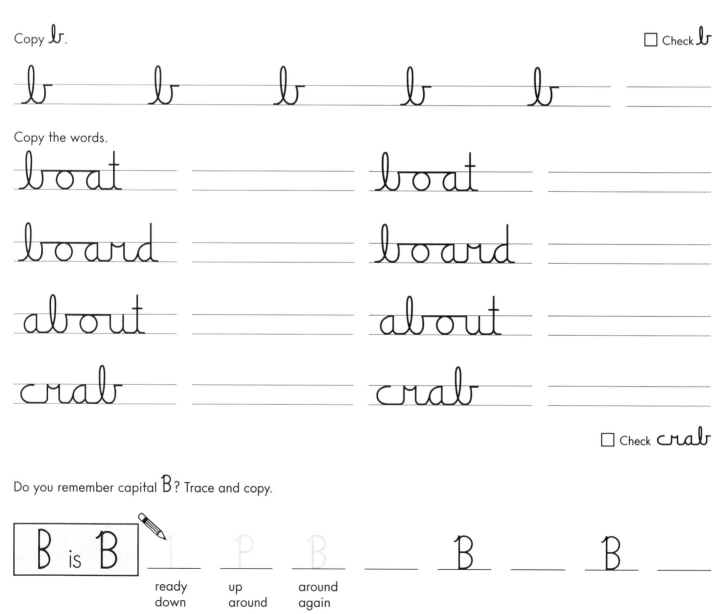

Copy ♭.   ☐ Check ♭

b   b   b   b   b

Copy the words.

boat _____   boat _____

board _____   board _____

about _____   about _____

crab _____   crab _____

☐ Check crab

Do you remember capital B? Trace and copy.

B is B

ready   up   around   B   B
down   around   again

v is ⋁

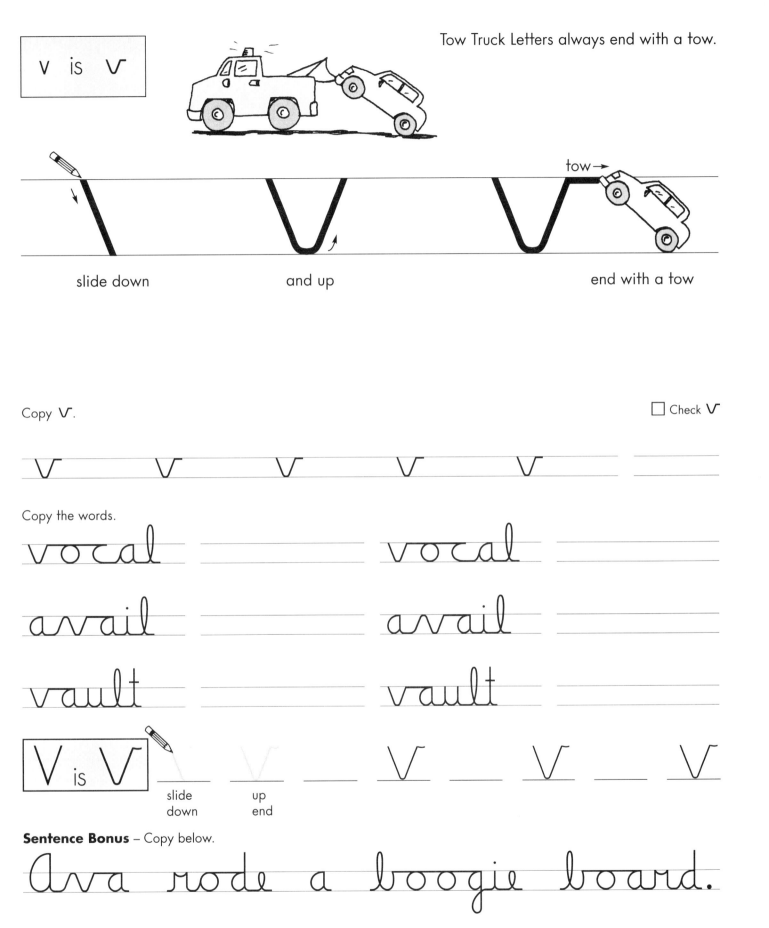

Tow Truck Letters always end with a tow.

tow →

slide down · and up · end with a tow

Copy ⋁.

☐ Check ⋁

⋁   ⋁   ⋁   ⋁   ⋁

Copy the words.

vocal   vocal

avail   avail

vault   vault

V is V

slide
down

up
end

V   V   V

Sentence Bonus – Copy below.

Ava rode a boogie board.

☐ Check Sentence

Tow Truck Connections

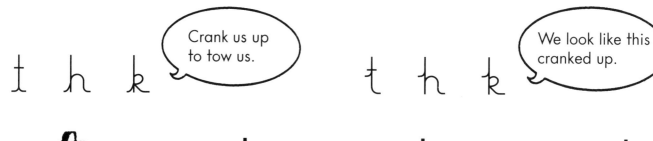

Copy the models.

t   t   pot   hot   rot

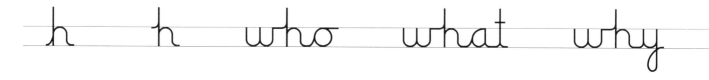

h   h   who   what   why

k   k   joke   look   took

Tow Truck Connections

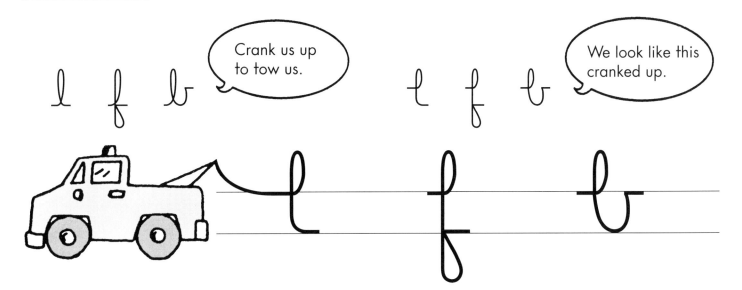

Copy the models.

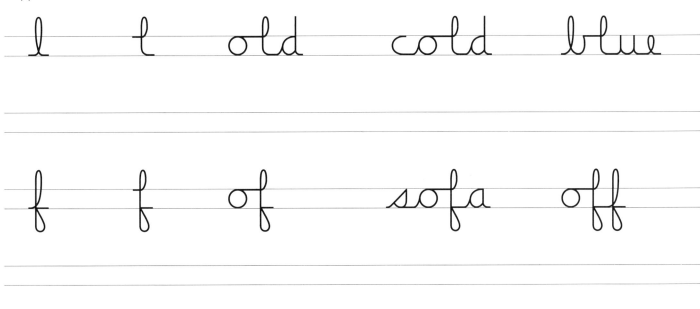

Tow Truck Connections

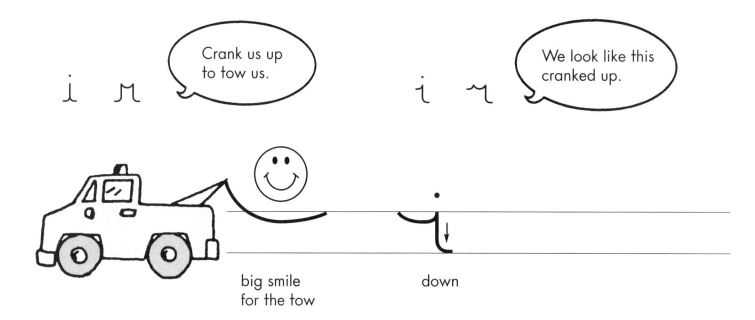

Crank us up to tow us.

We look like this cranked up.

big smile for the tow

down

Copy the models.

i i i oil bite wish

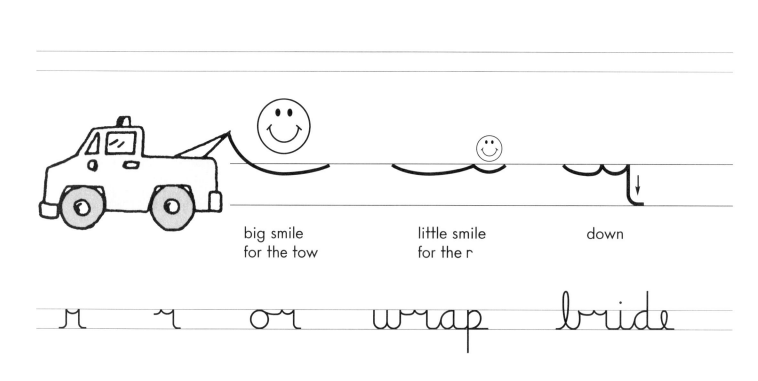

big smile for the tow

little smile for the r

down

n n n or wrap bride

Tow Truck Connections

Crank us up to tow us.

We look like this cranked up.

big smile
for the tow

turn and down

Copy the models.

l e we bed $veto$

big smile
for the tow

down
J-turn

touch the smile
travel away

s s $lost$ $jaws$ $ribs$

Cursive Success

Review & Mastery: Cursive to Cursive

a b c d e f g h i j k l m

m o p q r s t u v w x y z

Wait for the teacher to play The Freeze Game.

able - table

ride - bride

bull - bully

local - vocal

over - cover

took - book

soup - group

love - shove

gold - fold

best - vest

tightrope   apostrophe   political

See — Teacher's Guide page 90.

be → be

Translate print into cursive.
For lines 11 and 12, make new words with letters you've learned.

1. o w b v   o w b v

2. be

3. bus

4. echo

5. jewel

6. driver

7. hopeful

8. football

9. beautiful

10. vocabulary

11.

12.

above, a-b-o-v-e

Wait for the teacher to spell the words.
Write the Silly Spelling Words in cursive.

1.

2.

3.

4.

5.

6.

7.

8.

9.

10.

Extreme Challenge

m is m

↓ mule

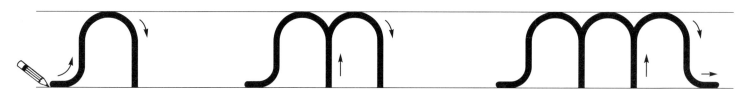

travel
up and over
down

up and over
down

again
travel away

(m has three humps)

Copy m.

m   m   m

Copy the words.

me   me

same   same

him   him

mule   mule

Do you remember capital M? Trace and copy.

M is m

ready
down

up, over
down

again

m   m

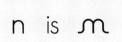 n is m

 ↓ violin

travel
up and over
down

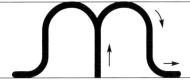

again
travel away

(m has two humps)

Copy m.   ☐ Check m

m   m   m   m

Copy the words.

mot   mot

might   might

know   know

violin   violin

☐ Check violin

Do you remember capital N? Trace and copy.

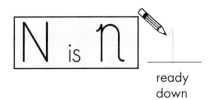 N is n      n   n   n

ready   up, over
down   down

Cursive Success

SPECIAL SITUATION

After a Tow Truck Letter, use printed m.

After a Tow Truck Letter, use **printed** m.

(m has two humps)

Copy m.   ☐ Check m

m   m   m   m

Copy the words.

come   come

prom   prom

from   from

some   some

home   home

☐ Check home

SPECIAL SITUATION

After a Tow Truck Letter, use printed n.

After a Tow Truck Letter, use **printed** n.

(n has one hump)

Copy n.   ☐ Check n

n   n   n   n   n   _____

Copy the words.

only   only

once   once

clown   clown

Sentence Bonus – Copy below.

Jon runs marathons.

☐ Check Sentence

a b c d e f g h i j k l m
n o p q r s t u v w x y z

Wait for the teacher to play The Freeze Game.

ring - sing   tone - phone

thin - think   pen - open

fame - blame   new - knew

when - then   nice - mice

song - long   now - snow

vacation   motorcycle   natural

See — Teacher's Guide page 96.

my → my

Translate print into cursive.
For lines 11 and 12, make new words with letters you've learned.

1. m   n   m   n
2. my
3. man
4. navy
5. nature
6. saving
7. machine
8. interest
9. submarine
10. navigation
11.
12.

none, n-o-n-e

Wait for the teacher to spell the words.
Write the Silly Spelling Words in cursive.

1.
2.
3.
4.
5.
6.
7.
8.
9.
10.

Extreme Challenge

x is *x* or **x**

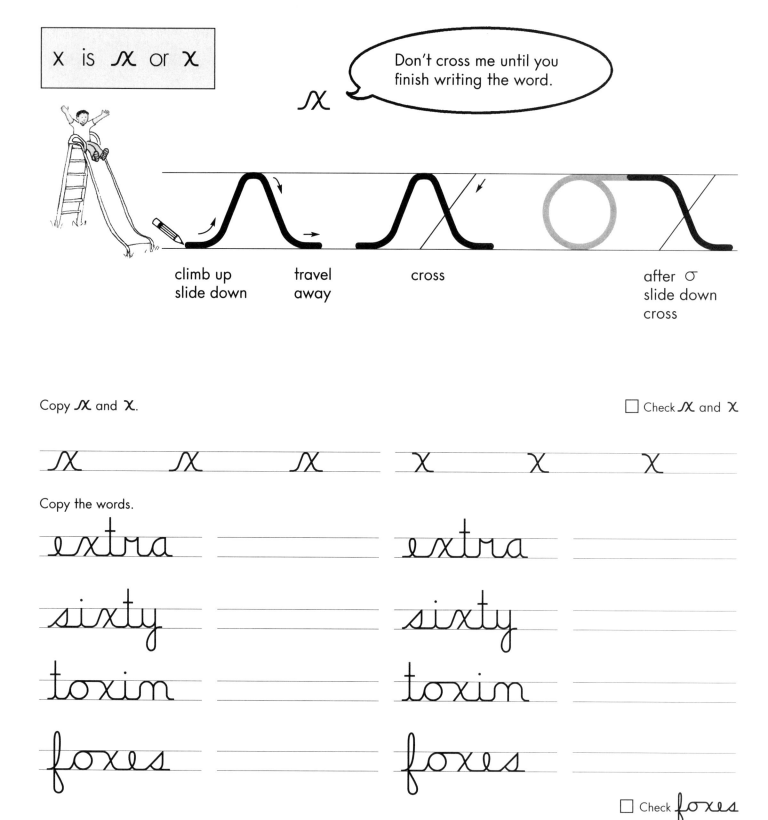

Don't cross me until you finish writing the word.

climb up
slide down

travel
away

cross

after o
slide down
cross

Copy *x* and **x**.

☐ Check *x* and **x**

Copy the words.

extra   extra

sixty   sixty

toxin   toxin

foxes   foxes

☐ Check foxes

Do you remember capital X? Trace and copy.

X is X

slide
down

cross
down

X   X   X

q is q

Here's how to make c into q.

bump

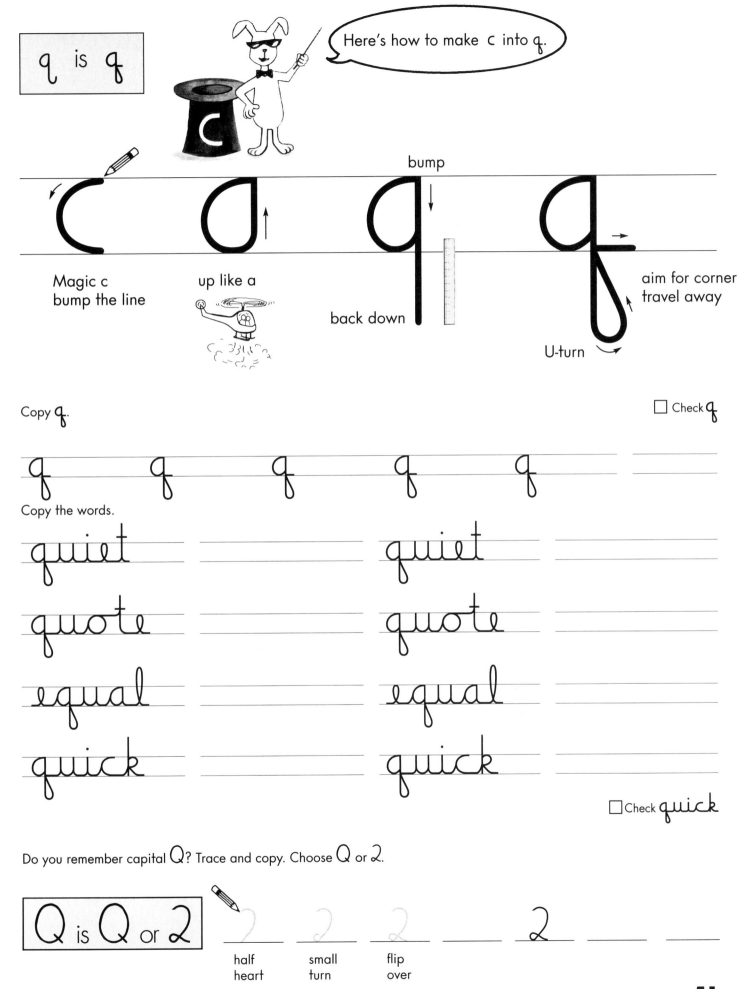

Magic c
bump the line

up like a

back down

U-turn

aim for corner
travel away

Copy q.

☐ Check q

q   q   q   q   q

Copy the words.

quiet   quiet

quote   quote

equal   equal

quick   quick

☐ Check quick

Do you remember capital Q? Trace and copy. Choose Q or 2.

Q is Q or 2   2   2   2   2

half
heart

small
turn

flip
over

z is *z*

Here's a heart.   My half   Your half

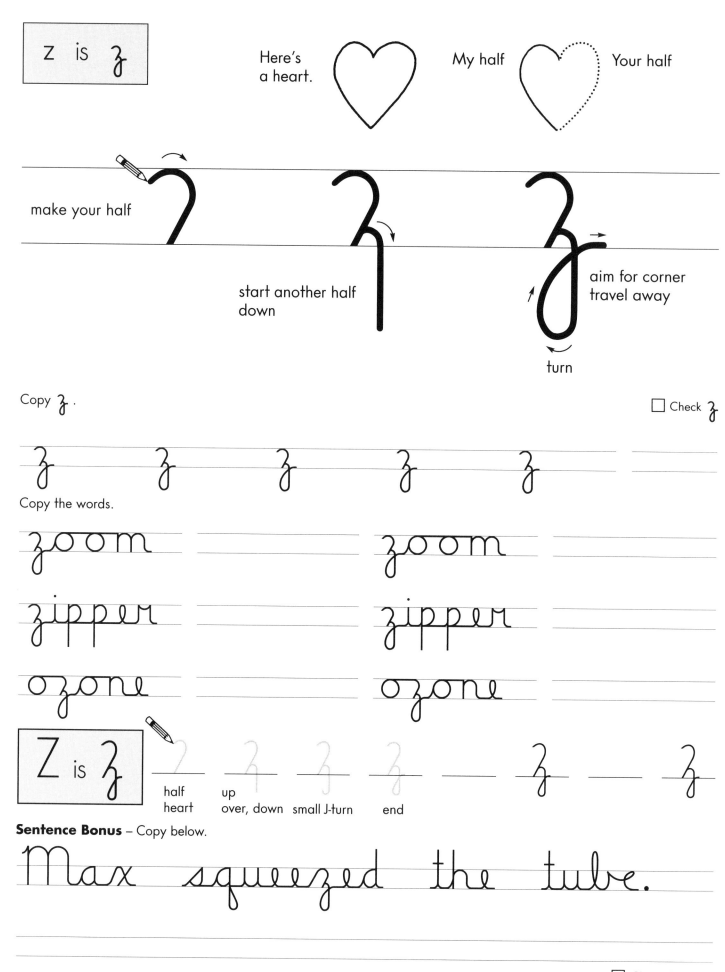

make your half

start another half down

aim for corner travel away

turn

Copy *z* .

☐ Check *z*

Copy the words.

zoom   zoom

zipper   zipper

ozone   ozone

Z is *z*

half heart   up over, down   small J-turn   end

Sentence Bonus – Copy below.

Max squeezed the tube.

☐ Check Sentence

TRANSLATE SENTENCES

Do you wonder if you should connect the capital to the next letter? You don't always connect them. Connect the capitals that end on the base line on the right side. Each sentence has at least one capital that connects and one that doesn't.

Translate these printed sentences into cursive.

Quinn walked the Appalachian Trail through West Virginia.

_____

_____

Zoinks! Is this a word you would find in the dictionary or on TV?

_____

_____

Is Montana as far north as North Dakota?

_____

_____

Xandra traveled to Ottawa in Ontario, Canada.

_____

_____

Blackbeard the Pirate's real name was Edward Teach.

_____

_____

Review & Mastery: Cursive to Cursive

a b c d e f g h i j k l m
n o p q r s t u v w x y z

Wait for the teacher to play The Freeze Game.

exit — extra

quick — quack

tax — fax

maze — amaze

box — fox

fizz — pizza

zoo — zoom

lax — relax

aqua — quail

zen — zenith

example   memorize   zoology

See — Teacher's Guide page 102.

Print to Cursive	Spelling to Cursive

ex → *ex*

quiz, q-u-i-z

Translate print into cursive.
For lines 11 and 12, make new words with letters you've learned.

Wait for the teacher to spell the words.
Write the Silly Spelling Words in cursive.

1. x q z   *x q z*

1. _____

2. ex

2. _____

3. zip

3. _____

4. jazz

4. _____

5. queen

5. _____

6. excuse

6. _____

7. extreme

7. _____

8. question

8. _____

9. aquaplane

9. _____

10. experiment

10. _____

11.

Extreme Challenge

12.

CAPITALS

Here are the capital letters. Beside each capital letter is another capital, the capital of a country.

Trace the steps.

Copy the capitals and capitals.

Magic C	up	back down

a a Athens

ready down	up around	around again

B B Beijing

Magic C

C C Canberra

down small turn	flip over	curve up end

D D Dakar

c in the air   c again

E E Edinburgh

ready down	J-turn	cross

F F Freetown

Trace the steps.

Copy the capitals and capitals.

curve up | top like ℓ+i | down big J-turn | end

𝒢 𝒢 Georgetown

ready down | down | up over | end

H H Havana

curve up | down J-turn | end

𝓘 𝓘 Islamabad

curve up | straight down | small J-turn | end

𝒥 𝒥 Jerusalem

ready down | kick! | slide down

K K Kabul

start like ℓ in the air | down small turn | flip over

𝓛 𝓛 Lima

ready down | up over down | again

M M Moscow

CAPITALS

Trace the steps.

ready
down

up
over
down

Magic C

keep on
going

end

ready
down

up
around

or

half
heart

small
turn

flip
over

ready
down

up
around

slide
down

straight
jet takeoff

print S

end

ready
down

J-turn

Copy the capitals and capitals.

N N   Nairobi

O O   Ottawa

P P   Paris

Q 2   Quito

R R   Rome

S S   Santiago

T T   Tokyo

Trace the steps.

Copy the capitals and capitals.

U U

down
travel
up

back
down

U U   Ulaanbaatar

V

slide
down

up
end

V V   Vienna

U W W

down
travel
up

again

end

W   Washington, D.C.

X

slide
down

cross
down

X X X X X X

U Y Y Y

down
travel
up

back
down

small
J-turn

end

Y Y   Yerevan

Z Z Z Z

half
heart

up
over
down

small
J-turn

end

Z Z   Zagreb

ALLITERATION

a B C D E F G H I J K L M
N O P Q R S ⓉJ U V W X Y Z

Choose your six favorite letters. Circle them.
Now write a fun sentence to feature each letter.

J   Jamiko tasted teriyaki in Jokyo.

COMPOUND WORDS

Fill in the blanks to make compound words.

 lady + _bug_ = _ladybug_

 _____ + _shoe_ = _____

 _____ + _ball_ = _____

 _____ + _nail_ = _____

 _____ + _light_ = _____

 _____ + _knob_ = _____

 _____ + _brow_ = _____

 _____ + _case_ = _____

 _____ + _chair_ = _____

 _____ + _room_ = _____

Galileo
1564-1642

Go to Italy! See the Leaning

Tower of Pisa. People say that's where

Galileo dropped two cannon balls,

one heavy, one light, to see which

one would land first.

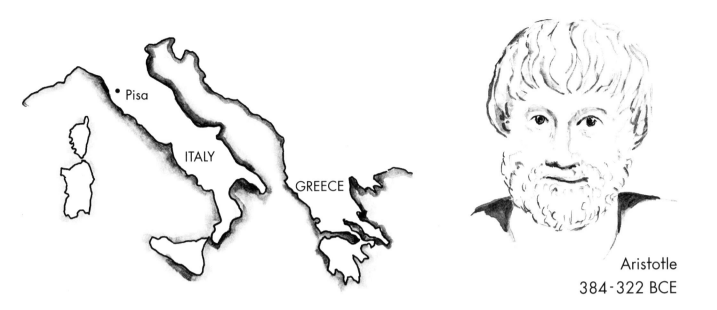

Aristotle
384-322 BCE

For centuries people believed

Aristotle, the Greek philosopher who

claimed that the heavier one would

land first. Galileo proved him wrong.

They landed together. That's physics!

SYNONYMS

Synonyms are words that share the same, or almost the same, meaning.
Synonym starts with s, just like same and similar.

Learn Greek:

syn   same
onym   name or word

automobile   car   vehicle

Translate each printed word into cursive.
Write a synonym beside it.

automobile   *automobile*   =   *car*

boat   =

cheerful   =

elderly   =

intelligent   =

purchase   =

street   =

student   =

woman   =

ANTONYMS

Antonyms are words that mean the opposite.

Learn Greek:

ant against
onym name or word

short

long

Translate each printed word into cursive.
Write an antonym beside it.

difficult   *difficult*   ≠   *easy*

expensive   ≠

chilly   ≠

generous   ≠

interesting   ≠

Write two sentences.
Use antonyms in each sentence.
For example: My grandfather is **old**, but my baby brother is **young**.

1.

2.

2013 Handwriting Without Tears®

Cursive Success **65**

PARAGRAPHS

Here comes the band! Sections

march in order to give the best

sound. High, small instruments are

in front of lower and louder ones.

Flutes are in front of the clarinets;

trumpets are ahead of the trombones

and tubas. The drums in the back

and the major in front set the rhythm.

Look at the band! Flags wave.

Uniforms are colorful. Players march in

lines with even rows, stepping together.

It's fun to see and hear the band.

HOMONYMS

Homonyms are words that have the same sound and the same spelling. Homonyms have different meanings. Dictionaries list and number the different meanings.

wave   wave

Write a sentence for each homonym.
Example: Sam's mom said, "**Wave** good-bye."
            He saw a **wave** in the ocean.

bat -

bat -

bug -

bug -

hide -

hide -

seal -

seal -

ring -

ring -

Homophones are words that have the same sound, but have different meanings and spellings.

see   sea

Homophones

Eye and I, see and sea,

Won and one, ate and eight,

So and sew, knew and new,

Homophones are fun to ~~dew~~ do.

     Cursive Success   **69**

PARAGRAPH - DRAFT

Draft a paragraph.

1. Tell your reader what you're going to say. That's your topic.

My topic:

2. Say it. List ideas or information about your topic. Don't use complete sentences, just get down your ideas.

About my topic:

-
-
-
-
-
-

3. Finish by telling your reader what you said in different words.

My topic restated:

PARAGRAPH - WRITE

Use your draft to write a paragraph. Remember to indent the first sentence.

Contractions are shortened forms of words. **Apostrophes** take the place of an omitted letter or letters.

Take Out!

I could write "do not," but I don't,

I could write "will not," but I won't,

I like contractions, they're fun to do,

Take out a letter, or take out a few!

Write out the long form of these contractions in cursive.

we're	we are	I'm
doesn't		you're
isn't		he'd
don't		she's
haven't		it's

SIMILES

Similes compare two things that are not really alike, but share a common feature. Similes use the words **like** or **as**.

- **as** a rock
- **like** a dream
- **like** a monkey
- **as** a feather
- **like** a fish
- **as** molasses

Complete each sentence with a simile from the above list.

Charlie swims _____ .

This bed is as hard _____ .

He climbs _____ .

I can lift it. It's as light _____ .

Hurry up! You're as slow _____ .

This car drives _____ .

METAPHORS

Metaphors are figures of speech. Metaphors actually say one thing is something else in order to describe it better.

Copy.

🚗 = 🍋   That car is a lemon!

 = 🎂   That test was a piece of cake.

PROVERBS

Proverbs are sayings that tell a truth.

Write the meaning.

A stitch in time saves nine.

A penny saved is a penny earned.

The early bird gets the worm.

Rome wasn't built in a day.

Never judge a book by its cover.

Libraries organize their books.

Biographies are shelved alphabetically by the subject's name. Fiction is by the author's name. Non-fiction uses a set of numbers, the Dewey Decimal system.

Wait for the teacher. Fill in the categories.

000 General Knowledge	500
100	600
200	700
300	800
400	900 Geography, History

See — Teacher's Guide page 127.

TOW TRUCK CONNECTIONS

o w b v

Copy the connections.

wh   wa

bo   or   ve

bl   ow   ol

bl   bb   be

wa   bl   oo   od

ol   be

br   bo   ov   ve

Copy the words.

whales   walrus

born   live

blow   holes

blubber

warm - blooded

cold   polar   bear

breathe   above

PARAGRAPH

Seals bark, whales sing, and

polar bears roar. They are social

marine mammals. They live in

groups and care for their young.

Fur or blubber keeps them warm,

even in the coldest water. These

mammals have adapted to marine life.

MNEMONICS

Mnemonics are memory aids. You can remember a sentence to remember the planets.
In 2006, astronomers decided that Pluto was not a planet. So, now there are only eight planets.

Copy.

Mercury   Venus   Earth   Mars

My   Very   Excited   Mother

Make up a mnemonic sentence.

m   V   E   m

ACRONYMS

Acronyms are words made from the initial letters of other words.

Copy.

SCUBA is an acronym for:

S Self   C Contained   U Underwater

Jupiter   Saturn   Uranus   Neptune

Jumped   Straight   Up   North.

J   S   U   n

B Breathing   A Apparatus

DICTIONARY DEFINITIONS

Directions:

1. Look up each word.

2. On the first line, write the part of speech.
   The dictionary uses abbreviations for the parts
   of speech. Here is the key:

   n.   = *noun*
   adj. = *adjective*
   v.   = *verb*
   adv. = *adverb*

3. On the second line, write the definition.

beet

Draw

beetle

amp = *noun*

a unit of electricity

ample =

beet =

beetle =

sing =

single =

© 2013 Handwriting Without Tears®

PARAGRAPH

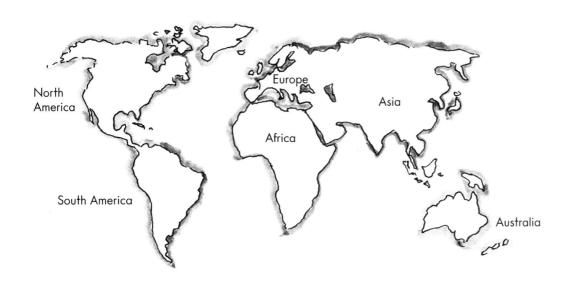

North
America

Europe

Asia

Africa

South America

Australia

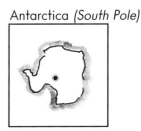

Antarctica *(South Pole)*

Do you know the continents?

Two are islands: Australia and Antarctica.

There are two Americas: North and South.

The last three are Asia, Africa, and Europe.

Six start with or use an A. One starts with E.

NAMES

Some capitals connect and some don't. Connect the capitals that end on the base line and on the right side. Connect these capitals to the next letter:

a C E J K L M n *2 R U y z

Your choice:
1. Translate these printed names into cursive.   OR   2. Write different names that start with the same capital.

Ann _____ _____   Noah _____ _____

Christopher _____   *Quentin _____

Ella _____ _____   Ryan _____ _____

Jake _____ _____   Uri _____ _____

Katherine _____   Yoko _____ _____

Loren _____ _____   Zachary _____

Matthew _____

DO NOT connect these capitals to the next letter:

B D F G H I O P S J V W X

Your choice:
1. Translate these printed names into cursive.   OR   2. Write different names that start with the same capital.

Brad _____ _____   Peter _____ _____

David _____ _____   Samantha _____

Frances _____ _____   Thomas _____ _____

Greg _____ _____   Virginia _____

Hans _____ _____   William _____ _____

Ingrid _____ _____   Xavier _____ _____

Oscar _____

*Note: 2 - this version of capital Q would connect.   Q - this version of capital Q would not connect.

THANK YOU

Write a thank you letter. Organize your letter like this.

Date
Month Day, Year

Greeting
Dear _____ ,

Body
    Say thank you and tell how much you appreciate the gift or help. Mention what it is or what they did. Add details to make it more personal.

Use a comma:
1. After the day of the month
2. After the greeting
3. After the closing

Closing
Sincerely, Thank you, or Love,

Signature

GREEK & LATIN

Use Greek and Latin to figure out big words.

Copy.

PREFIXES

equi-, sym- = same

quad- = 4

kilo- = 1,000

dia- = through

rect- = right

WORD ROOTS

later = side

meter = measure

equation

quadrilateral

kilometer

diameter

rectangle

equilateral

symmetry

PARAGRAPH

We measure dimensions. String

has one dimension: length. Flat

shapes have two: length and width.

Solid shapes have three dimensions:

length, width, and height.

List two-dimensional shapes. □ ○ △

1. _____

2. _____

3. _____

4. _____

5. _____

List three-dimensional shapes.

1. _____

2. _____

3. _____

4. _____

5. _____

inches   1   2   3   4   5   6

People first began measuring with

their bodies. They measured thickness

with thumbs, horses with hands, boards

with feet, and cloth with an arm.

These measurements became standardized.

Fill in the blanks with the missing unit of measurement.

4 inches   =   1 hand

12 inches   =   1 _____

36 inches   =   3 _____   =   1 _____

5,280 feet   =   1 _____

PARAGRAPH

The metric system of measurement

developed as math and science

advanced. The basic unit is the meter.

Smaller and larger units are in

decimals or multiples of ten.

Wait for the teacher. Write the metric words.

1 m

1 cm

1 km

1 mm

CAPITALS

CAPITALIZE: Finish the sentences about yourself.

Initials   My initials are _____. _____. _____.

Names   My name is _____ .

Days   Today is _____ .

Months   My birthday is in _____ .

Languages   I speak _____ .

Holidays   My favorite holiday is _____ .

People   I admire _____ .

Places   I would like to visit _____ .

CAPITALS

Draw your teacher.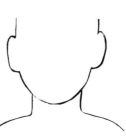

CAPITALIZE: Finish the sentences about yourself.

Schools   My school is _____.

*Titles, names   My teacher is _____.

*Book titles   I read _____.

*Movie titles   I saw _____.

*Song titles   I can sing _____.

Cities, towns   I live in _____.

Rivers, lakes,   The closest water is _____.
oceans

First word   I said, " _____. "
of a quote

*Capitalize the first, last, and important words in titles.

Cursive Success **89**

PARAGRAPHS

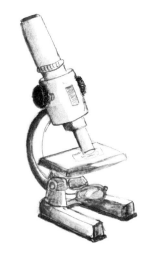
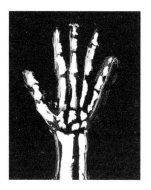
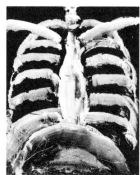
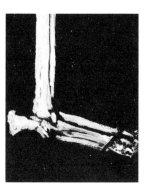

Finish paragraphs 2 and 3.

Think of washing machines, electric lights, cell phones, jets, and computers. Those inventions changed how people live, but two inventions did more. They made a life or death difference.

Before the microscope was invented, doctors didn't know that germs made people sick.

Before X-rays were invented, doctors couldn't look inside people's bodies.

QUOTATIONS

Quotations are a person's exact words.

All the world's a stage.

William Shakespeare
1564 - 1616

Copy the famous quotes like this:

William Shakespeare said, "All the world's a stage."

If there is no struggle, there is no progress.

Frederick Douglass
1818 - 1895

What we play is life.

Louis Armstrong
1901 - 1971

Despite everything, I believe people are really good at heart.

Anne Frank
1929 - 1945

_____

_____

That's one small step for man, one giant leap for mankind.

Neil Armstrong
1930 - 2012

_____

_____

WHAT DID THEY MEAN?

Remember, we learned that a metaphor is a figure of speech. There are three metaphors in these quotations. Discuss them in your class.

"All the world's a stage."   How can the world be a stage?

"What we play is life."   How could a trumpet play life?

"That's...one giant leap for mankind."   How could mankind take a leap?

     Cursive Success

Graduation

by Sherry Landes

I used to think cursive was confusing

I look back now and that's amusing

I learned it's easy to connect each letter

Now, I write faster and my work looks better.

Translate the poem into cursive, or make up your own cursive poem.